THE POPULAR YOUTUBE CHANNEL, QUIZ BOSS, BRINGS YOU:
WOULD YOU RATHER & MORE!

THIS BOOK WILL HAVE YOU ANSWERING QUESTIONS ABOUT YOUR CLOSEST FRIENDS, YOUR DREAM VACATIONS, SPOOKIEST FEARS AND EVEN DISGUSTING GROSS-OUT QUESTIONS!

OVER 350 HILARIOUS, SILLY & CHALLENGING QUESTIONS TO MAKE YOU LAUGH!

Table of Contents

1. WOULD YOU RATHER......................PAGE 3

2. OKAY BESTIE!................................PAGE 23

3. ALL AOUT ME................................PAGE 45

4. NEVER HAVE I EVER......................PAGE 67

5. PICK IT OR KICK IT........................PAGE 89

6. GROSSER THAN GROSS..................PAGE 101

1. WHICH WOULD YOU CHOOSE AT A FAIR?
   ◯ DEEP FRIED TWINKIE   ● CHURRO

2. WHICH WOULD YOU RATHER EAT?
   ◯ CREME BRULEE   ● FLAN

3. WHICH DESSERT DO YOU PREFER?
   ◯ PEANUT BUTTER BARS   ● LEMON BARS

4. WOULD YOU RATHER INDULGE IN?
   ● CUP OF HOT CHOCOLATE   ◯ S'MORES

Would you Rather?

1. WOULD YOU RATHER LIVE THE REST OF YOUR LIFE:
   - 🟢 ALONE ON AN ISLAND
   - ⚪ IN OUTER SPACE

2. WOULD YOU RATHER HAVE:
   - ⚪ CEREAL THAT SMELLS LIKE FEET
   - 🟢 FEET THAT SMELL LIKE CEREAL

3. WOULD YOU RATHER:
   - 🟢 TAKE A FIELD TRIP TO A FARM
   - ⚪ TAKE A WHOLE FARM ON YOUR FIELD TRIP

4. WHICH ANIMAL WOULD YOU RATHER BE?
   - 🟢 A FAST-RUNNING SLOTH
   - ⚪ SLOW-MOTION CHEETAH

Would you Rather?

1. WOULD YOU RATHER GO WITH YOUR FRIENDS ON:
   ◯ FLYING AIRPLANE RIDE   ◯ SPINNING TEACUPS

2. WHICH WOULD YOU RATHER DO AT THE FAIR?
   ◯ THE GIANT SUPERSLIDE   ◯ BUMPER CARS

3. WHICH FAIR GAME ARE YOU PLAYING?
   ◯ BALL TOSS GAME   ◯ BASKETBALL

4. AT NIGHT WOULD YOU RATHER WATCH:
   ◯ THE ELECTRICAL PARADE   ◯ FIREWORKS SHOW

Would you Rather?

1. WHICH WOULD YOU RATHER FIND IN YOUR BED?
- ● A COCKROACH
- ○ A HAIRY SPIDER

2. WHICH WOULD YOU RATHER FIND IN YOUR ATTIC?
- ○ A PORCELAIN DOLL
- ● A BLACK CAT

3. WHICH WOULD YOU RATHER LISTEN TO ALL NIGHT?
- ● A THUNDERSTORM
- ○ ANGRY DOGS

4. WHICH WOULD YOU RATHER TOUCH?
- ● EARTHWORMS
- ○ SLUGS

Would you Rather?

1. WHICH PET WOULD YOU RATHER HAVE?
   - ○ A HAMSTER-SIZED ELEPHANT
   - ○ ELEPHANT-SIZED HAMSTER

2. WOULD YOU RATHER EAT:
   - ○ ICE CREAM THAT TASTES LIKE MEATBALLS
   - ○ MEATBALLS THAT TASTE LIKE ICE CREAM

3. WHICH PET WOULD YOU RATHER HAVE?
   - ○ A LADYBUG-SIZED KITTEN
   - ○ A KITTEN-SIZED LADYBUG

4. WHICH ANIMAL WOULD YOU RATHER HAVE?
   - ○ A CAT THAT BARKS LIKE A DOG
   - ○ DOG THAT MEOWS LIKE A CAT

Would you Rather?

1. WOULD YOU RATHER PLAY:
   ◯ SPORTS WITH FRIENDS   ◯ VIDEO GAMES

2. WOULD YOU RATHER EAT:
   ◯ POTATO CHIPS   ◯ FRENCH FRIES

3. WOULD YOU RATHER GO:
   ◯ SCUBA DIVING   ◯ SKYDIVING

4. WOULD YOU RATHER SMELL:
   ◯ STINKY SOCKS   ◯ OLD CHEESE

Would you Rather?

1. WOULD YOU RATHER EAT:
◯ BANANA PUDDING   ◯ PECAN PIE

2. WOULD YOU RATHER EAT:
◯ STRAWBERRY SHORTCAKE ◯ CHERRY TART

3. WOULD YOU RATHER EAT:
◯ MOON CAKE   ◯ MOCHI

4. WOULD YOU RATHER EAT:
◯ ICE CREAM CONE   ◯ CUPCAKES

1. WOULD YOU RATHER EAT:
   ◯ FRENCH BREAD PIZZA   ◯ SLOPPY JOES

2. WOULD YOU RATHER SNACK ON:
   ◯ CHEESE AND CRACKERS   ◯ GRANOLA BAR

3. WOULD YOU RATHER GRAB ON THE GO:
   ◯ AN UNCRUSTABLE   ◯ A HOT POCKET

4. WOULD YOU RATHER SNACK ON:
   ◯ FRUIT ROLL-UP   ◯ FRUIT SNACKS

Would you Rather?

1. WOULD YOU RATHER:
   ◯ RUN A MILE   ◯ DO YOGA

2. WHICH MOVIE SNACK IS BETTER?
   ◯ POPCORN   ◯ NACHOS

3. WOULD YOU RATHER GO ON VACATION TO:
   ◯ DISNEYLAND   ◯ HAWAII

4. WOULD YOU RATHER:
   ◯ HAVE FIVE SIBLINGS ◯ BE AN ONLY CHILD

1. WOULD YOU RATHER RIDE:
   ◯ FERRIS WHEEL   ◯ CAROUSEL

2. WOULD YOU RATHER GO ON THE:
   ◯ TRAIN RIDE   ◯ SKY BUCKETS

3. WOULD YOU RATHER GET SPLASHED IN A:
   ◯ LAZY RIVER   ◯ WATERSLIDE

4. WOULD YOU RATHER GO ON A:
   ◯ ROLLER COASTER LOOP ◯ FREE FALL DROP

1. WHAT TYPE OF PARTY DO YOU LIKE MORE?
   ◯ SLUMBER PARTY   ◯ LASER TAG

2. WHAT ARE YOU DOING ON VACATION?
   ◯ LOUNGING BY THE POOL   ◯ ATV ADVENTURE

3. ON A SATURDAY NIGHT YOU'D RATHER:
   ◯ HANG OUT WITH FRIENDS   ◯ READ A BOOK

4. WOULD YOU RATHER GO:
   ◯ ROLLER SKATING   ◯ SKATEBOARDING

Would you Rather?

1. WOULD YOU RATHER WATCH:
   ○ FUNNY TV SHOWS
   ○ FUNNY VIDEOS ON YOUR PHONE

2. WOULD YOU RATHER WEAR:
   ○ COZY SLIPPERS
   ○ COWBOY BOOTS

3. WOULD YOU RATHER EAT:
   ○ A PIZZA COVERED IN M&MS
   ○ A HOT DOG COVERED IN WHIPPED CREAM

4. WOULD YOU RATHER:
   ○ PLAY FLAG FOOTBALL
   ○ GO BOWLING

Would you Rather?

1. WHICH WOULD YOU RATHER SEE IN YOUR BEDROOM?
   - ◯ A TOY MOVING ON ITS OWN
   - ◯ A SPOOKY GHOST

2. WHERE WOULD YOU RATHER SPEND THE NIGHT?
   - ◯ A HAUNTED HOUSE
   - ◯ A GRAVEYARD

3. HOW WOULD YOU RATHER SPEND HALLOWEEN?
   - ◯ GO TRICK-OR-TREATING
   - ◯ PASS OUT CANDY

4. WHICH WOULD YOU RATHER WEAR FOR HALLOWEEN?
   - ◯ A SPOOKY COSTUME
   - ◯ FUNNY COSTUME

1. WOULD YOU RATHER HANG OUT AT A:
○ SUPER LOUD LIBRARY   ○ REALLY QUIET CONCERT

2. WOULD YOU RATHER EAT A:
○ SUGARY CHEESEBURGER   ○ SALTY CUPCAKE

3. WOULD YOU RATHER BECOME FRIENDS WITH:
○ AN ALIEN VISITNG EARTH   ○ BIG FOOT

4. WHICH ANIMAL WOULD YOU RATHER HAVE?
○ AN OTTER LIVING IN YOUR BATHTUB   ○ A GIRAFFE LIVING IN YOUR BACKYARD

Would you Rather?

1. WOULD YOU RATHER WATCH:
◯ HORROR FILMS   ◯ ROMANCE MOVIES

2. WOULD YOU RATHER WEAR:
◯ COMFY CLOTHES   ◯ TRENDY CLOTHES

3. WOULD YOU RATHER EAT:
◯ A BURGER THAT TASTES LIKE GUMMY BEARS   ◯ GUMMY BEARS THAT TASTE LIKE A BURGER

4. WOULD YOU RATHER:
◯ PLAY MINIATURE GOLF   ◯ GO TO AN ESCAPE ROOM

1. WOULD YOU RATHER EAT:
   ◯ TURKEY SANDWICH   ◯ PB&J SANDWICH

2. WOULD YOU RATHER EAT:
   ◯ COOL RANCH DORITOS   ◯ NACHO DORITOS

3. WOULD YOU RATHER EAT:
   ◯ CHOCOLATE CHIP COOKIES   ◯ BROWNIES

4. WOULD YOU RATHER EAT:
   ◯ CHEESEBURGER MEAL   ◯ NUGGET MEAL

Would you Rather?

1. WHICH PET WOULD YOU RATHER HAVE?
   - ○ A SCALY GUINEA PIG
   - ○ A FURRY GOLDFISH

2. WOULD YOU RATHER EAT:
   - ○ A HOT BOWL OF ICE CREAM
   - ○ A COLD BOWL OF SOUP

3. WOULD YOU RATHER GO TO SCHOOL WEARING:
   - ○ SHOES ON YOUR HEAD
   - ○ HATS ON YOUR FEET

4. WOULD YOU RATHER:
   - ○ HAVE FRECKLES ON YOUR FACE
   - ○ DRAW FACES ON YOUR FRECKLES

Would you Rather?

1. WOULD YOU RATHER EAT:
   ◯ YOUR PARENTS' COOKING   ◯ AT A RESTAURANT

2. WOULD YOU RATHER:
   ◯ GET UP EARLY   ◯ SLEEP IN

3. WOULD YOU RATHER WATCH:
   ◯ DISNEY+   ◯ NETFLIX

4. WOULD YOU RATHER ADOPT:
   ◯ KITTEN   ◯ PUPPY

okay Bestie!

Who is most likely to do the following things—YOU or your BESTIE?

1. WHO SINGS THE LOUDEST IN THE CAR?
   - ◯ ME
   - ● MY BESTIE

2. WHO IS GOOD AT SAVING MONEY?
   - ● ME
   - ◯ MY BESTIE

3. WHO CAN STAY UP ALL NIGHT WITHOUT SLEEPING?
   - ● ME
   - ◯ MY BESTIE

4. WHO IS MOST LIKELY TO WEAR SHORTS WHEN IT'S COLD OUTSIDE?
   - ◯ ME
   - ● MY BESTIE

Who is most likely to do the following things—
YOU or your BESTIE?

1. GET A PERFECT SCORE ON A MATH QUIZ?
    ME   ◯ MY BESTIE

2. EAT PINEAPPLE ON PIZZA?
   ◯ ME   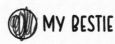 MY BESTIE

3. GETS A SONG STUCK IN THEIR HEAD ALL DAY?
   ◯ ME   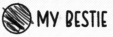 MY BESTIE

4. HAS A PLAYLIST THEY LISTEN TO BEFORE GAMES OR BIG EVENTS?
    ME   ◯ MY BESTIE

okay Bestie!

*Who is most likely to do the following things—
YOU or your BESTIE?*

1. WHO GETS MORE EXCITED FOR HOLIDAYS?
   - ⬤ ME
   - ◯ MY BESTIE

2. ARE EITHER OF YOU DOUBLE JOINTED?
   - ◯ ME   ⊗   ◯ MY BESTIE

3. WHO'S MORE SCARED OF SPIDERS?
   - ⬤ ME
   - ⬤ MY BESTIE

4. WHO IS MOST LIKELY TO PUSH SOMEONE IN A POOL?
   - ⬤ ME
   - ◯ MY BESTIE

okay Bestie!

Who is most likely to do the following things— YOU or your BESTIE?

1. WRITE AND DIRECT A MOVIE?
    ME   ◯ MY BESTIE

2. BE PRESIDENT ONE DAY?
    ME   ◯ MY BESTIE

3. TRIP AND FALL IN FRONT OF THE CLASS?
   ◯ ME    MY BESTIE

4. RECYCLE THEIR SODA CAN?
    ME   ◯ MY BESTIE

okay Bestie!

Who is most likely to do the following things— YOU or your BESTIE?

1. WHO'S WAKING UP EARLY TO EXERCISE?
   ⊙ ME 　　　　⊗　　　● MY BESTIE

2. WHO'S WAKING UP EARLY TO DO THEIR MAKEUP?
   ⊙ ME 　　　　　　　● MY BESTIE

3. WHO'S MOST LIKELY TO GO AWAY TO COLLEGE?
   ● ME 　　　　　　　⊙ MY BESTIE

4. WHO WOULD GO ON AN AROUND-THE-WORLD CRUISE?
   ● ME 　　　　　　　● MY BESTIE

okay Bestie!

Who is most likely to do the following things— YOU or your BESTIE?

1. WHO'S THE SWEETEST?
   ● ME   ○ MY BESTIE

2. WHO SPENDS THE MOST TIME ON THEIR HAIR?
   ● ME   ○ MY BESTIE

3. WHO WANTS TO GET THE LEAD IN THE SCHOOL PLAY?
   ○ ME   ● MY BESTIE

4. WHO LAUGHS THE LOUDEST AT THEIR OWN JOKES?
   ○ ME   ● MY BESTIE

Who is most likely to do the following things— YOU or your BESTIE?

1. WHO'S MORE LIKELY TO PULL A PRANK IN CLASS?
   ◯ ME   ● MY BESTIE

2. WHO'S MOST LIKELY TO KEEP A SECRET?
   ◯ ME   ◯ MY BESTIE

3. WHO'S MOST LIKELY TO RESCUE A STRAY CAT?
   ● ME   ● MY BESTIE

4. WHO'S MOST LIKELY TO WIN AN ARGUMENT WITH THEIR PARENTS?
   ◯ ME   ● MY BESTIE

Who is most likely to do the following things— YOU or your BESTIE?

1. WHO'S BEST WITH DIRECTIONS?

   ● ME   ○ MY BESTIE

2. WHO'S ALWAYS RUNNING LATE?

   ○ ME   ● MY BESTIE

3. WHO WOULD ORDER STEAK INSTEAD OF PIZZA?

   ● ME   ● MY BESTIE

4. WHO GETS BRAIN FREEZE FROM EATING ICE CREAM?

   ● ME   ● MY BESTIE

okay Bestie!

Who is most likely to do the following things— YOU or your BESTIE?

1. WHO IS TEACHER'S PET?
   - ⬤ ME
   - ◯ MY BESTIE

2. WHO WOULD DYE THEIR HAIR PURPLE?
   - ◯ ME
   - (X)
   - ◯ MY BESTIE

3. WHO GETS IN TROUBLE FOR TALKING IN CLASS?
   - ⬤ ME
   - ⬤ MY BESTIE

4. WHO IS MOST LIKELY TO LAUGH DURING A SERIOUS MOMENT?
   - ⬤ ME
   - ⬤ MY BESTIE

Who is most likely to do the following things— YOU or your BESTIE?

1. WHO'S MOST LIKELY TO GO TO A PERFORMING ARTS SCHOOL?
   ○ ME   ● MY BESTIE

2. WHO IS MOST LIKELY TO BEAT A VIDEO GAME?
   ● ME   ○ MY BESTIE

3. WHO MESSAGES BACK THE FASTEST?
   ✗ ME   ✗ MY BESTIE

4. WHO ALWAYS WANTS TO SIT IN THE FRONT SEAT OF THE ROLLERCOASTER?
   ○ ME   ✗ MY BESTIE

Who is most likely to do the following things—
YOU or your BESTIE?

1. WHO CAN DO A PERFECT CARTWHEEL?
   ○ ME   ● MY BESTIE

2. WHO IS MOST LIKELY TO CRY DURING A SAD MOVIE?
   ○ ME ✗   ○ MY BESTIE

3. WHO WOULD EAT CALAMARI?
   ○ ME   ● MY BESTIE

4. WHO IS MOST LIKELY TO START THEIR OWN BUSINESS ONE DAY?
   ● ME   ○ MY BESTIE

Who is most likely to do the following things—
YOU or your BESTIE?

1. WHO'S MOST LIKELY TO KNOW TIKTOK DANCES?
   ○ ME   ● MY BESTIE

2. WHO'S FIRST ON THE DANCE FLOOR?
   ● ME   ● MY BESTIE

3. WHO'S MOST LIKELY TO MOVE TO A BIG CITY AFTER HIGH SCHOOL?
   ○ ME   ● MY BESTIE

4. WHO WOULD SPEND THE NIGHT ALONE IN A HAUNTED MANSION FOR $1,000?
   ● ME   ● MY BESTIE

Who is most likely to do the following things— YOU or your BESTIE?

1. WHO WOULD EAT DOG FOOD ON A DARE?
   ● ME   ○ MY BESTIE

2. WHO WOULD WANT TO BE A POP STAR?
   ○ ME   ● MY BESTIE

3. WHO WOULD AUDITION FOR A BAKING SHOW?
   ○ ME   ● MY BESTIE

4. WHO WOULD WANT TO BE THE FIRST KID IN OUTER SPACE?
   ● ME   ○ MY BESTIE

okay Bestie!
Who is most likely to do the following things—
YOU or your BESTIE?

1. WHO MAKES THE FUNNIEST FACES?
   ◯ ME   ◯ MY BESTIE

2. WHO IS THE WORST LIAR?
   ◯ ME   ◯ MY BESTIE

3. WHO COULD EAT A WHOLE PIZZA BY THEMSELF?
   ◯ ME   ◯ MY BESTIE

4. WHO FALLS ASLEEP WATCHING A MOVIE?
   ◯ ME   ◯ MY BESTIE

okay Bestie!

Who is most likely to do the following things— YOU or your BESTIE?

1. WHO'S THE NEXT TAYLOR SWIFT?
   - ◯ ME
   - ◯ MY BESTIE

2. WHO GIVES GREAT ADVICE WHEN THEIR FRIENDS ARE SAD?
   - ◯ ME
   - ◯ MY BESTIE

3. WHO HAS THE MOST ORGANIZED BACKPACK OR SCHOOL LOCKER?
   - ◯ ME
   - ◯ MY BESTIE

4. WHO IS MORE LIKELY TO GET VOTED CLASS PRESIDENT AT SCHOOL?
   - ◯ ME
   - ◯ MY BESTIE

okay Bestie!

Who is most likely to do the following things—
YOU or your BESTIE?

1. WHO WOULD BINGE WATCH A WHOLE SERIES IN ONE DAY?
   ◯ ME   ◯ MY BESTIE

2. WHO'S THE LAST ONE TO FINISH EATING LUNCH?
   ◯ ME   ◯ MY BESTIE

3. ARE EITHER OF YOU LEFT HANDED?
   ◯ ME   ◯ MY BESTIE

4. WHO IS MOST LIKELY TO WRITE THE NEXT HARRY POTTER?
   ◯ ME   ◯ MY BESTIE

okay Bestie!

Who is most likely to do the following things—YOU or your BESTIE?

1. WHO CHECKS THEIR HOROSCOPE EVERYDAY?
   - ○ ME
   - ○ MY BESTIE

2. KNOWS THE MOST ABOUT SUPERHEROES?
   - ○ ME
   - ○ MY BESTIE

3. WHO SLEEPS IN THE LATEST?
   - ○ ME
   - ○ MY BESTIE

4. WHO HAS THE BIGGER SWEET TOOTH?
   - ○ ME
   - ○ MY BESTIE

okay Bestie!

Who is most likely to do the following things— YOU or your BESTIE?

1. WHO'S THE LOUDEST?
   ○ ME   ○ MY BESTIE

2. WHO FALLS ASLEEP THE FASTEST?
   ○ ME   ○ MY BESTIE

3. WHO'S THE MOST DRAMATIC?
   ○ ME   ○ MY BESTIE

4. WHO'S MOST LIKELY TO LOSE THEIR STUFF?
   ○ ME   ○ MY BESTIE

Who is most likely to do the following things— YOU or your BESTIE?

1. WHO'S MOST LIKELY TO FORGET THEIR FRIEND'S BIRTHDAY?
   ○ ME   ○ MY BESTIE

2. WHO'S THE PICKIEST EATER?
   ○ ME   ○ MY BESTIE

3. WHO IS MORE OF A MORNING PERSON?
   ○ ME   ○ MY BESTIE

4. WHO'S MOST LIKELY TO GET A TATTOO WHEN THEY'RE OLDER?
   ○ ME   ○ MY BESTIE

Who is most likely to do the following things— YOU or your BESTIE?

1. WHO'S MOST LIKELY TO GET FAMOUS?
   ○ ME   ○ MY BESTIE

2. WHO'S MOST LIKELY TO WIN A MILLION DOLLARS?
   ○ ME   ○ MY BESTIE

3. WHO WILL BECOME A PROFESSIONAL ATHLETE?
   ○ ME   ○ MY BESTIE

4. WHO SENDS THE MOST TEXTS?
   ○ ME   ○ MY BESTIE

all about me!

1. ONE WORD MY BEST FRIEND WOULD USE TO DESCRIBE ME: _____

2. I'M A GOOD COOK:
   ◯ YES   ◯ NO

3. I SNORE:
   ◯ YES   ◯ NO

4. MY NICKNAME / NICKNAMES:
   _____
   _____

1. THE COUNTRY I'D MOST LIKE TO VISIT IS:
   _____

2. IF I COULD CHOOSE ANY CELEBRITY TO GO ON VACATION WITH, IT WOULD BE:
   _____

3. THE TWO FRIENDS I'D LIKE TO GO ON A CRUISE WITH ARE:
   _____

4. THE FRIEND I'VE KNOWN THE LONGEST IS:
   _____

all about me!
True or False Time!

1. I ALWAYS BRUSH MY TEETH BEFORE I GO TO BED:
   ○ TRUE   ○ FALSE:

2. I PREFER SHOWERS OVER BATHS:
   ○ TRUE   ○ FALSE

3. I'D RATHER WEAR A DRESS THAN WEAR PANTS:
   ○ TRUE   ○ FALSE

4. I REMEMBER TO CHARGE MY ELECTRONICS EVERY DAY:
   ○ TRUE   ○ FALSE

True or False Time!

1. I'VE WON A MEDAL OR TROPHY BEFORE:
   ○ TRUE   ○ FALSE

2. I'VE WORN A SOCK WITH A HOLE IN IT TO SCHOOL BEFORE:
   ○ TRUE   ○ FALSE

3. I'VE ACCIDENTALLY FARTED IN CLASS:
   ○ TRUE   ○ FALSE

4. I HAVE AN EMBARRASSING NICKNAME THAT NO ONE KNOWS ABOUT:
   ○ TRUE   ○ FALSE

all about me!

1. I'M AFRAID OF THE DARK WHEN I'M BY MYSELF:
   ◯ YES   ◯ NO

2. I SLEEP WITH A TEDDY BEAR OR STUFFIE:
   ◯ YES   ◯ NO

3. I SLEEP WITH SOCKS ON:
   ◯ YES   ◯ NO

4. I SLEEP WITH THE TV ON:
   ◯ YES   ◯ NO

all about me!

1. MY MIDDLE NAME IS:

_____

2. I AM NAMED AFTER SOMEONE IN MY FAMILY:
   ◯ YES   ◯ NO

3. THE BEST PRANK I'VE EVER PLAYED ON SOMEONE:

_____

4. DID THEY KNOW IT WAS YOU WHO PRANKED THEM?
   ◯ YES   ◯ NO

all about me!

1. I'M A GOOD SINGER:
  ◯ YES   ◯ NO
  ◯ I ONLY SING IN THE SHOWER

2. MY "CELEBRITY NAME" IS:
  (COMBINE YOUR MIDDLE NAME AND THE FIRST STREET YOU LIVED ON)

  _____

3. I TALK IN MY SLEEP:
  ◯ YES   ◯ NO

4. MY DREAM CAREER IS:

  _____

all about me!

1. MY FIRST PET WAS A HAMSTER:
   ◯ YES   ◯ NO

2. I CAN DO A CARTWHEEL:
   ◯ YES   ◯ NO

3. I CAN WRITE WITH MY LEFT HAND:
   ◯ YES   ◯ NO

4. I CRY EASILY DURING SAD MOVIES:
   ◯ YES   ◯ NO

all about me!

1. IF I HAD TO EAT ONE VEGETABLE FOR THE REST OF MY LIFE, IT WOULD BE:

   _____

2. TWO FOODS I COMBINE AND EAT TOGETHER THAT MY FRIENDS THINK ARE WEIRD:

   _____ & _____

3. THE DRINK THAT I ORDER AT RESTAURANTS:

   _____

4. FOOD THAT I ABSOLUTELY CANNOT LIVE WITHOUT:

   _____

all about me!

1. THE THING I'M MOST AFRAID OF:

   _____

2. I PICK MY NOSE WHEN NO ONE IS LOOKING?
   - ◯ YES
   - ◯ NO

3. I WIPE MY BOOGERS ON THE WALL:
   - ◯ YES
   - ◯ NO
   - ◯ EEEEEEEWWWWW GROSS!

4. THE GROSSEST FOOD I'VE EVER TRIED:

   _____

all about me!

1. MY BIRTH MONTH IS:

_____

2. MY FIRST PET'S NAME:

_____

3. I'M MORE OF A:
　○ MORNING PERSON　　○ NIGHT OWL

4. I LOVE RAINY DAYS:
　○ YES　　○ NO

all about me!

1. I LIKE TO TALK TO ANIMALS MORE THAN PEOPLE:
   ◯ YES   ◯ NO

2. I'VE SEEN A DOUBLE RAINBOW BEFORE:
   ◯ YES   ◯ NO

3. I'VE GONE BACKWARDS DOWN A WATERSLIDE:
   ◯ YES   ◯ NO

4. I'VE GONE ZIPLINING BEFORE:
   ◯ YES   ◯ NO

all about me!

1. I ALWAYS PUT HOT SAUCE ON MY FOOD:
   ○ TRUE   ○ FALSE

2. I'VE EATEN OR TRIED WASABI
   ○ TRUE   ○ FALSE

3. I AM:
   ○ SUPER CLEAN   ○ A MESSY MESS

4. THE LAST BOOK I READ:

_____

all about me!

1. I PREFER DOGS OVER CATS:
   ○ YES   ○ NO

2. MY ASTROLOGICAL BIRTH SIGN IS:

   _____

3. I HAVE ALLERGIES:
   ○ YES   ○ NO
   MY ALLERGIES ARE: _____

4. IF I WAS A COLOR, I'D BE:

   _____

all about me!

1. THE CITY I WANT TO LIVE IN WHEN I'M OLDER IS:

   _____

2. IF I COULD TRAVEL BACK IN TIME AND REPEAT ONE GRADE, IT WOULD BE:

   _____

3. IF I COULD TRAVEL TO THE FUTURE, I'D WANT TO BE THIS AGE:

   _____

4. IF I COULD HAVE ONE WISH, IT WOULD BE:

   _____

1. I KNOW ALL THE WORDS TO THE STAR-SPANGLED BANNER:
   ◯ TRUE   ◯ FALSE

2. I LIKE TO PAINT MY TOENAILS:
   ◯ TRUE   ◯ FALSE

3. I'VE STAYED UP PAST MIDNIGHT BEFORE:
   ◯ TRUE   ◯ FALSE

4. I'VE TOUCHED A DOLPHIN BEFORE:
   ◯ TRUE   ◯ FALSE

all about me!

1. THE ONE THING THAT I AM THE BEST AT IS:

   _____

2. I'M MORE OF A INTROVERT THAN EXTROVERT:
   - ○ YES
   - ○ NO

3. THE SUPERHERO THAT IS MOST LIKE ME IS:

   _____

   WHY? _____

4. MY FAVORITE SEASON IS:
   - ○ WINTER
   - ○ SUMMER
   - ○ SPRING
   - ○ FALL

all about me!

1. MY FAVORITE TYPE OF FOOD IS:

   _____

2. MY LEAST FAVORITE FOOD IS:

   _____

3. MY FAVORITE SMELL IS:

   _____

4. MY LEAST FAVORITE SMELL IS:

   _____

1. I'VE TRAVELED TO ANOTHER COUNTRY:
   ◯ YES   ◯ NO

2. I PREFER PLANE TRIPS OVER CAR TRIPS:
   ◯ YES   ◯ NO

3. I'VE GOTTEN HURT PLAYING A SPORT:
   ◯ YES   ◯ NO

4. I'VE BROKEN A BONE BEFORE:
   ◯ YES   ◯ NO

all about me!

1. MY FAVORITE TV SHOW RIGHT NOW IS:
   _____

2. I BELIEVE THAT ALIENS EXIST:
   ◯ YES   ◯ NO

3. IF I COULD CHANGE MY NAME, I WOULD CHOOSE:
   _____

4. I AM MORE:
   ◯ CREATIVE   ◯ PRACTICAL

never have I ever!

Never Have I Ever!

1. EVER RECORDED SILLY VIDEOS ON YOUR PARENT'S PHONE WITHOUT THEM KNOWING?
   - ◯ HAVE
   - ◯ HAVEN'T

2. HAVE YOU EVER TRIPPED OVER YOUR OWN FEET?
   - ◯ HAVE
   - ◯ HAVEN'T

3. EVER WALKED INTO A GLASS DOOR BECAUSE YOU DIDN'T SEE IT?
   - ◯ HAVE
   - ◯ HAVEN'T

4. EVER WAVED BACK AT SOMEONE WHO WASN'T ACTUALLY WAVING AT YOU?
   - ◯ HAVE
   - ◯ HAVEN'T

1. EVER WRITTEN SECRETS DOWN IN A DIARY?
   ○ HAVE   ○ HAVEN'T

2. HAVE YOU EVER WORN PAJAMAS ALL DAY LONG?
   ○ HAVE   ○ HAVEN'T

3. HIT THE SNOOZE BUTTON MORE THAN ONCE?
   ○ HAVE   ○ HAVEN'T

4. EVER EATEN BREAKFAST FOR DINNER?
   ○ HAVE   ○ HAVEN'T

Never Have I Ever!

1. HAVE YOU EVER KNOCKED OVER A DRINK AT A RESTAURANT?
   - ○ HAVE
   - ○ HAVEN'T

2. EVER EATEN ALL YOUR HALLOWEEN CANDY IN ONE NIGHT?
   - ○ HAVE
   - ○ HAVEN'T

3. HAVE YOU EVER PASSED A NOTE IN CLASS?
   - ○ HAVE
   - ○ HAVEN'T

4. HAVE YOU EVER CUT YOUR OWN HAIR?
   - ○ HAVE
   - ○ HAVEN'T

1. HAVE YOU EVER BEEN ON AN AIRPLANE?
   ◯ HAVE   ◯ HAVEN'T

2. EVER TRAVELED OUT OF THE COUNTRY?
   ◯ HAVE   ◯ HAVEN'T

3. HAVE YOU EVER GONE SNORKELING?
   ◯ HAVE   ◯ HAVEN'T

4. EVER BEEN ON A FAMILY BEACH VACATION?
   ◯ HAVE   ◯ HAVEN'T

Never Have I Ever!

1. EVER EATEN THE LAST OF A SNACK AND PUT THE EMPTY BOX BACK?
   ○ HAVE   ○ HAVEN'T

2. HAVE YOU EVER FORGOTTEN YOUR FRIEND'S BIRTHDAY?
   ○ HAVE   ○ HAVEN'T

3. EVER PLAYED BAREFOOT IN THE RAIN?
   ○ HAVE   ○ HAVEN'T

4. EVER ACCIDENTALLY USED SALT INSTEAD OF SUGAR WHEN BAKING?
   ○ HAVE   ○ HAVEN'T

Never Have I Ever!

1. EVER TURNED OFF A HORROR MOVIE BECAUSE IT WAS TOO SCARY?
   - ○ HAVE
   - ○ HAVEN'T

2. HAVE YOU EATEN COLD PIZZA STRAIGHT FROM THE FRIDGE?
   - ○ HAVE
   - ○ HAVEN'T

3. EVER DANCED AROUND THE HOUSE TO KIDZ BOP?
   - ○ HAVE
   - ○ HAVEN'T

4. EVER BURNED COOKIES BY ACCIDENTALLY COOKING THEM TOO LONG?
   - ○ HAVE
   - ○ HAVEN'T

Never Have I Ever!

1. EVER PRETENDED TO BE ASLEEP TO GET OUT OF DOING CHORES?
   - ◯ HAVE
   - ◯ HAVEN'T

2. EVER GOTTEN BUBBLEGUM STUCK IN YOUR HAIR?
   - ◯ HAVE
   - ◯ HAVEN'T

3. EVER GOTTEN A HORRIBLE HAIRCUT?
   - ◯ HAVE
   - ◯ HAVEN'T

4. EVER DRAWN ON SOMEONE'S FACE WHILE THEY WERE SLEEPING?
   - ◯ HAVE
   - ◯ HAVEN'T

Never Have I Ever!

1. EVER SENT A TEXT OR MESSAGE TO THE WRONG PERSON ON ACCIDENT?
   ○ HAVE   ○ HAVEN'T

2. HAVE YOU EVER SLEPT IN A TENT ON A CAMPING TRIP?
   ○ HAVE   ○ HAVEN'T

3. EVER MADE S'MORES OVER A CAMPFIRE?
   ○ HAVE   ○ HAVEN'T

4. HAVE YOU EVER TAKEN A CUTE SELFIE WITH AN ANIMAL?
   ○ HAVE   ○ HAVEN'T

Never Have I Ever!

1. EVER THOUGHT YOU SAW A UFO?
   ○ HAVE   ○ HAVEN'T

2. HAVE YOU SEEN A TORNADO?
   ○ HAVE   ○ HAVEN'T

3. EVER RAN UPSTAIRS QUICKLY AT NIGHT BECAUSE YOU FELT LIKE SOMETHING WAS BEHIND YOU?
   ○ HAVE   ○ HAVEN'T

4. EVER SHOVED STUFF IN YOUR CLOSET WHEN YOU WERE SUPPOSED TO BE CLEANING YOUR ROOM?
   ○ HAVE   ○ HAVEN'T

Never Have I Ever!

1. HAVE YOU EVER FORGOTTEN YOUR SCHOOL LUNCH AT HOME?
   ○ HAVE   ○ HAVEN'T

2. EVER TRIED SUSHI?
   ○ HAVE   ○ HAVEN'T

3. HAVE YOU EVER TRIED SASHIMI (RAW FISH)?
   ○ HAVE   ○ HAVEN'T

4. EVER DIPPED FRENCH FRIES IN ICE CREAM?
   ○ HAVE   ○ HAVEN'T

Never Have I Ever!

1. EVER TASTED DOG FOOD JUST TO SEE WHAT IT TASTES LIKE?
   ○ HAVE   ○ HAVEN'T

2. HAVE YOU EVER BEEN CAUGHT MAKING FACES AT SOMEONE BEHIND THEIR BACK?
   ○ HAVE   ○ HAVEN'T

3. EVER TOLD A SECRET THAT YOU WEREN'T SUPPOSED TO TELL?
   ○ HAVE   ○ HAVEN'T

4. HAVE YOU EVER SCREAMED ON A ROLLER COASTER?
   ○ HAVE   ○ HAVEN'T

1. HAVE YOU EVER DRANK MILK STRAIGHT FROM THE CARTON?
   ◯ HAVE   ◯ HAVEN'T

2. HAVE YOU EVER FOUND A STRAY ANIMAL AND MADE IT YOUR PET?
   ◯ HAVE   ◯ HAVEN'T

3. EVER ACCIDENTALLY EATEN SOMETHING EXPIRED?
   ◯ HAVE   ◯ HAVEN'T

4. EVER WATCHED PRESCHOOL CARTOONS WHEN YOU'RE OLDER BECAUSE YOU STILL LIKE THEM?
   ◯ HAVE   ◯ HAVEN'T

Never Have I Ever!

1. EVER WORN A SCARY COSTUME ON HALLOWEEN?
   ○ HAVE   ○ HAVEN'T

2. FOUND A SPIDER IN YOUR ROOM?
   ○ HAVE   ○ HAVEN'T

3. EVER SPENT THE NIGHT IN A HOSPITAL?
   ○ HAVE   ○ HAVEN'T

4. EVER WORN YOUR SHOES ACCIDENTALLY ON THE WRONG FEET TO SCHOOL?
   ○ HAVE   ○ HAVEN'T

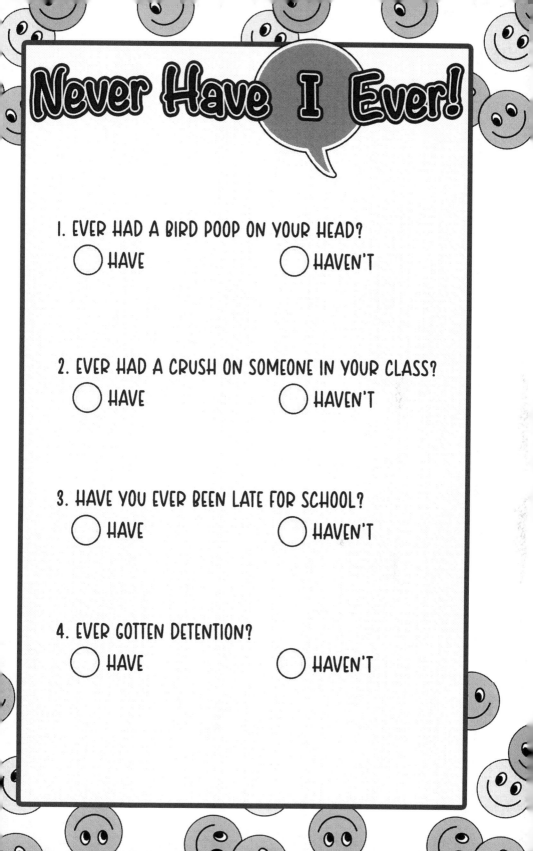

Never Have I Ever!

1. EVER HAD A BIRD POOP ON YOUR HEAD?
   ○ HAVE   ○ HAVEN'T

2. EVER HAD A CRUSH ON SOMEONE IN YOUR CLASS?
   ○ HAVE   ○ HAVEN'T

3. HAVE YOU EVER BEEN LATE FOR SCHOOL?
   ○ HAVE   ○ HAVEN'T

4. EVER GOTTEN DETENTION?
   ○ HAVE   ○ HAVEN'T

1. HAVE YOU EVER GONE ON A TRIP TO DISNEYLAND OR DISNEY WORLD?
   ◯ HAVE   ◯ HAVEN'T

2. HAVE YOU EVER TRIED SURFING OR BODYBOARDING?
   ◯ HAVE   ◯ HAVEN'T

3. EVER PEED IN A POOL?
   ◯ HAVE   ◯ HAVEN'T

4. HAVE YOU EVER GOTTEN CAUGHT TALKING TO YOURSELF IN PUBLIC?
   ◯ HAVE   ◯ HAVEN'T

Never Have I Ever!

1. HAVE YOU EVER DONE KARAOKE?
   ◯ HAVE   ◯ HAVEN'T

2. HAVE YOU EVER DANCED AT A WEDDING?
   ◯ HAVE   ◯ HAVEN'T

3. HAVE YOU EVER BEEN TO A SURPRISE PARTY?
   ◯ HAVE   ◯ HAVEN'T

4. HAVE YOU EVER GONE INTO A ROOM TO GET SOMETHING THEN FORGET WHAT YOU'RE THERE FOR?
   ◯ HAVE   ◯ HAVEN'T

Never Have I Ever!

1. EVER SANG AND DANCED IN THE MIRROR?
   ◯ HAVE   ◯ HAVEN'T

2. HAVE YOU EVER LAUGHED UNTIL YOU CRIED?
   ◯ HAVE   ◯ HAVEN'T

3. HAVE YOU EVER SEEN A SHOOTING STAR?
   ◯ HAVE   ◯ HAVEN'T

4. EVER PRETENDED TO LIKE A GIFT SO IT WOULDN'T HURT SOMEONE'S FEELINGS?
   ◯ HAVE   ◯ HAVEN'T

Never Have I Ever!

1. EVER MIXED TWO OR MORE TYPES OF SODA INTO ONE DRINK?
   - ◯ HAVE
   - ◯ HAVEN'T

2. HAVE YOU EVER HAD A CAVITY?
   - ◯ HAVE
   - ◯ HAVEN'T

3. HAVE YOU EVER EATEN A PLAIN LEMON?
   - ◯ HAVE
   - ◯ HAVEN'T

4. HAVE YOU MIXED TWO TYPES OF CEREAL IN ONE BOWL?
   - ◯ HAVE
   - ◯ HAVEN'T

Never Have I Ever!

1. EVER ACCIDENTALLY DROPPED SOMETHING IN THE TRASH CAN AND HAD TO DIG IT OUT?
   ◯ HAVE   ◯ HAVEN'T

2. HAVE YOU EVER TRIED BEING A VEGETARIAN?
   ◯ HAVE   ◯ HAVEN'T

3. EVER BEEN STUCK IN AN ELEVATOR?
   ◯ HAVE   ◯ HAVEN'T

4. EVER WATCHED TV FOR FOUR HOURS STRAIGHT?
   ◯ HAVE   ◯ HAVEN'T

Never Have I Ever!

1. EVER WORN THE SAME CLOTHES TWO DAYS IN ROW?
   - ◯ HAVE
   - ◯ HAVEN'T

2. HAVE YOU EVER FALLEN OUT OF BED?
   - ◯ HAVE
   - ◯ HAVEN'T

3. HAVE YOU EVER MOVED HOUSES?
   - ◯ HAVE
   - ◯ HAVEN'T

4. EVER BLOWN OUT SOMEONE ELSE'S BIRTHDAY CANDLES?
   - ◯ HAVE
   - ◯ HAVEN'T

pick it
or
kick it

Pick It or Kick It!

MOST LIKELY TO...
PICK WHICH OPTION YOU'RE MORE LIKELY TO DO

● SQUEEZE THE TOOTHPASTE FROM THE TOP   **OR**   ○ ROLL THE TOOTHPASTE FROM THE BOTTOM

○ GET UP EARLY IN THE MORNING   **OR**   ● STAY UP LATE AT NIGHT

○ COVER YOUR EYES DURING A SCARY MOVIE   **OR**   ● KEEP YOUR EYES WIDE OPEN

○ GIVE STUFF AWAY WHEN YOU'RE DONE WITH IT   **OR**   ○ KEEP EVERYTHING FOREVER

Pick It or Kick It!

ROAD TRIP SNACKS
PICK WHICH ONE YOU'D RATHER EAT

○ GOLDFISH CRACKERS　　OR　　○ PRETZELS

○ SLURPEE　　OR　　○ BILZZARD

○ PIZZA COMBO SNACKS　　OR　　○ CORN NUTS

○ TRAIL MIX　　OR　　○ POPCORN

HARDEST CHOICES EVER!
PICK WHICH OPTION YOU'D PREFER

○ HAVE A MILLION FOLLOWERS   **OR**   ○ WIN A MILLION DOLLARS

○ OWN A PRIVATE JET   **OR**   ○ OWN A SUPER YACHT

○ HAVE HARRY POTTER AS A BEST FRIEND   **OR**   ○ HAVE SPIDERMAN AS A BEST FRIEND

○ BE ABLE TO PLAY EVERY INSTRUMENT   **OR**   ○ BE ABLE TO SPEAK EVERY LANGUAGE

Pick It or Kick It!

FAVORITE PETS
PICK WHICH ANIMAL YOU'D RATHER HAVE FOR A PET

○ CHIHUAHUA   OR   ○ PIT BULL

○ GUINEA PIG   OR   ○ HAMSTER

○ OUTDOOR CAT OR   ○ INDOOR CAT

○ SNAKE   OR   ○ TURTLE

Pick It or Kick It!

MOST LIKELY TO...
PICK WHICH OPTION YOU'RE MORE LIKELY TO DO

○ SLEEP WITH YOUR FEET UNDER THE COVERS   **OR**   ○ SLEEP WITH YOUR FEET OUTSIDE OF THE COVERS

○ USE THE BATHROOM WITH THE DOOR OPEN   **OR**   ○ CLOSE THE DOOR FOR PRIVACY

○ TAKE A MILLION SELFIES   **OR**   ○ NOT A SELFIE PERSON

○ POUR YOUR MILK FIRST, AND THEN YOUR CEREAL   **OR**   ○ POUR YOUR CEREAL FIRST

Pick It or Kick It!

FOOD CHOICES
PICK WHICH OPTION YOU'D PREFER

◯ CHUNKY PEANUT BUTTER   OR   ◯ SMOOTH PEANUT BUTTER

◯ PUT PINEAPPLE ON PIZZA   OR   ◯ NEVER PUT PINEAPPLE ON PIZZA

◯ EAT THE CRUST ON YOUR SANDWICHES   OR   ◯ EAT YOUR SANDWICHES WITH NO CRUST

◯ EAT DESSERT FOR BREAKFAST OR   ◯ EAT BREAKFAST FOR DINNER

Pick It or Kick It!

ROAD TRIP SNACKS
PICK WHICH ONE YOU'D RATHER EAT

○ SOUR PATCH KIDS   OR   ○ SNICKERS

○ BEEF JERKY   OR   ○ SLIM JIMS

○ FLAMIN' HOT CHEETOS   OR   ○ TAKIS FUEGO

○ FUNYUNS   OR   ○ SUN CHIPS

Pick It or Kick It!

FAVORITE PETS
PICK WHICH ANIMAL YOU'D RATHER HAVE FOR A PET

○ PYGMY GOAT   OR   ○ TEACUP PIG

○ GOLDFISH   OR   ○ BETA FISH

○ LIZARD   OR   ○ PARROT

○ CHICKEN   OR   ○ RAT

HARDEST CHOICES EVER!
PICK WHICH OPTION YOU'D PREFER

○ GET A FACE TATTOO   OR   ○ HAVE A SHAVED HEAD FOREVER

○ NEVER TALK AGAIN   OR   ○ BURP EVERY TIME YOU TALK

○ LIVE SOMEWHERE WITH EARTHQUAKES   OR   ○ LIVE SOMEWHERE WITH HURRICANES

○ GET A SUNBURN EVERY TIME YOU GO TO THE BEACH   OR   ○ NEVER GO TO THE BEACH AGAIN

WHICH ONE ARE YOU?
PICK WHICH OPTION YOU RELATE TO MORE

○ CAREFULLY UNWRAP PRESENTS   **OR**   ○ TEAR PRESENTS OPEN

○ READ A REAL BOOK   **OR**   ○ READ ON A DEVICE

○ LOVE BEING THE CENTER OF ATTENTION   **OR**   ○ PREFER BEING BEHIND THE SCENES

○ SLEEP WITH THE TV ON   **OR**   ○ SLEEP IN COMPLETE SILENCE

grosser than gross

101

Pick which one is grosser!

1. ◯ KISS A COCKROACH   ◯ KISS A FROG

2. ◯ BE STUCK IN A ROOM FULL OF RATS   ◯ BE STUCK IN A ROOM FULL OF EARTHWORMS

3. ◯ NOT CHANGE YOUR SHIRT FOR A YEAR   ◯ NOT CHANGE YOUR SOCKS FOR A YEAR

4. ◯ SMELL MOLDY CHEESE   ◯ SMELL CURDLED MILK

Pick which one is grosser!

1. ○ HAVE A BABY THROW UP ON YOU   ○ CHANGE A BABY'S POOPY DIAPER

2. ○ SLEEP WITH SAND IN YOUR BED   ○ HAVE SAND STUCK BETWEEN YOUR TOES

3. ○ HAVE A BOOGER HANGING OUT OF YOUR NOSE ALL DAY   ○ WALK AROUND FARTING ALL DAY

4. ○ TOUCH A GOLDFISH   ○ PET A SALAMANDER

Grosser Than Gross?

Pick which one is grosser!

1. ○ HAVE A BUG FLY UP YOUR NOSE   ○ HAVE A BUG FLY INTO YOUR EAR

2. ○ SMELL YOUR FAMILY'S DIRTY FEET   ○ SMELL A SKUNK IN YOUR HOUSE

3. ○ CLEANING UP DOG POOP   ○ CLEANING A LITTER BOX

4. ○ EAT OYSTERS   ○ EAT CHOCOLATE COVERED CRICKETS

Pick which one is grosser!

1. ◯ EAT PICKLED EGGS   ◯ EAT FROG LEGS

2. ◯ EAT MUSTARD-FLAVORED ICE CREAM   ◯ EAT A TUNA FISH MILKSHAKE

3. ◯ EATING RAW FISH   ◯ EATING OLD FISH

4. ◯ NEVER USING DEODORANT   ◯ NEVER USING TOOTHPASTE

Pick which one is grosser!

1. ◯ DRINK POND WATER   ◯ EAT MUD

2. ◯ TOUCH SOMEONE'S EYE   ◯ TOUCH SOMEONE'S EAR WAX

3. ◯ PICK FOOD OUT OF YOUR TEETH IN PUBLIC   ◯ POP A PIMPLE IN PUBLIC

4. ◯ PICK UP SOMEONE'S BELLY BUTTON LINT   ◯ PICK UP SOMEONE'S SNOTTY TISSUE

FINISHED! DONE! FIN! FINITO!
You did it!

1. This book is property of: _____

2. The people I played this book with are:

   _____
   _____
   _____

3. The person whose answer surprised me the most:

   _____

4. The funniest answer:

   _____

5. How much I like this book:

   ◯ A little   ◯ A lot   ◯ I LOVEEEEED IT!

If you loved this Would You Rather Book then you will love the Quiz Boss: Slumber Party Book, coming soon.

Don't forget to follow us on social media, and find more of our books on **Amazon.com** *and at* **QuizBoss.co.**

Made in the USA
Middletown, DE
03 February 2024

48986968R00060